I0532579

Astro Power

FIVE REASONS MILLENNIALS
LOVE ASTROLOGY

- Ev Zervoudakis

Astro Power - FIVE Reasons Millennials Love Astrology

1st Edition

Holistic Healing Astrology

Loving Special Thanks

Sofia and Maria, my daughters who are my everything, who put up with me from day one!

Mary Whittle, my long-time friend, colleague, confidant, and soundboard. I love you!

Paul Brokaw at Brokaw Personalized Services, who made the impossible possible!

PROLOGUE

*Unlock the Secrets of the Stars
To Transform Your Life*

INTRODUCTION

Astrology has fascinated humanity for centuries, offering profound insights into our personalities, relationships, and life paths.

In "The ASTRO POWER: Five Reasons Millennials Love Astrology", we dive into the incredible world of astrology and explore why it holds the key to understanding ourselves and the universe around us. This captivating book will inspire and empower you to embark on a transformative journey of self-discovery, harnessing the power of astrology to unlock your full potential.

REASON 1

"Knowing yourself is the beginning of all wisdom."

— Aristotle.

DISCOVER YOUR TRUE SELF

Unveiling the mysteries of your birth chart, you'll uncover a wealth of information about your unique personality traits, strengths, and challenges. Learn how to decode the symbols and aspects in your chart and gain a deeper understanding of your true self. By embracing your authentic nature, you'll embark on a path of self-acceptance and personal growth.

REASON 2

"The meeting of two personalities is like the contact of two chemical substances: if there is any reaction, both are transformed."

— *Carl Gustav Jung*

NAVIGATE RELATIONSHIPS WITH CLARITY

Explore the fascinating realm of synastry and compatibility, discovering how astrology can shed light on your relationships with others.

By examining the cosmic connections between charts, you'll gain insights into compatibility, communication styles, and potential challenges. Empowered with this knowledge, you can build healthier and more fulfilling connections with loved ones, friends, and even colleagues.

REASON 3

"Timing is easy to predict through the movement of the stars as they give the propensity of pure potential."

— Ambika Devi

PREDICT THE FUTURE

Delve into the world of predictive astrology and learn how to anticipate and navigate the ebb and flow of life's events. Explore the powerful tools of transits, progressions, and solar returns to gain foresight into key life transitions and opportunities. By harnessing the predictive power of astrology, you can make informed decisions, align with cosmic energies, and maximize your potential for success and happiness.

REASON 4

"*Everything you do to improve your physical well-being will have a positive impact on how good you feel about yourself.*"

— *Brian Tracy*

ENHANCE YOUR WELL-BEING

Astrology goes beyond the realm of personality and relationships—it offers valuable insights into your physical, mental, and emotional well-being. Discover the connections between astrological signs, elements, and health indicators. Uncover effective self-care practices tailored to your unique astrological makeup and harness the cosmic energies for overall well-being and vitality.

REASON 5

"The two most important days in your life are the day you are born and the day you find out why."

— Mark Twain

ALIGN WITH YOUR LIFE PURPOSE

Unlock the secrets of your life purpose and soul's journey through astrology. By deciphering the nodal axis, Midheaven, and other key elements in your chart, you'll gain clarity on your true calling and the lessons you're meant to learn in this lifetime.

Embrace your cosmic blueprint, align with your passions, and manifest a life filled with purpose and fulfillment.

CONCLUSION

"The future belongs to those who believe in the beauty of their dreams."

– Eleanor Roosevelt

START YOUR JOURNEY

An illuminating guide that invites you to embark on a transformative journey of self-discovery. Embrace the power of astrology and unlock the secrets of the stars to gain profound insights, make informed decisions, and live a life aligned with your true self. Discover the limitless potential that lies within you and harness the transformative energy of astrology to create a brighter future.

ASTROLOGY BOOK SERIES

Embark on a transformative journey guided by Ev Zervoudakis's profound wisdom and knowledge and unlock the hidden mysteries of the universe to find your true purpose and inner truth. Discover her works and allow the invisible powers of the universe to become your ally on the path to personal growth, fulfillment, and happiness. Don't miss the opportunity to enrich your life through her extraordinary insights and wisdom.

Ev Zervoudakis's compassionate and insightful approach to spiritual guidance empowers individuals to tap into their inner wisdom and live abundantly. Ev's books are your gateway to a more joyful and fulfilled life.

With profound wisdom, honed through her role as a professional astrologer, mentor, and coach, helps countless souls unlock their full potential. Her unique approach emphasizes personal empowerment and self-awareness, making her a beacon of hope in an ever-changing world.

With Ev as your guide, the universe's invisible powers will become your ally in achieving personal growth, fulfillment, and happiness. Don't miss the opportunity to enrich your life through her extraordinary insights and wisdom.

FOLLOW HOLISTIC HEALING ASTROLOGY

 Website
holistichealingastrology.com

Book Appointment
holistichealingastrology.com/book-consultations/

Subscribe to keep in touch.
holistichealingastrology.com/newsletter/

Blog Post
holistichealingastrology.com/blog/

TikTok
tiktok.com/@holistichealingastrology

YouTube Channel
youtube.com/@holistichealingastrology

FaceBook
facebook.com/05051847730284

IG
instagram.com/holistichealingastrology